"Days Gone By- A look back on our lives"

By

Patricia Ann Leudeman – Chiappa

Dear Mom, Anthony, Aunt Mary, Aunt Maryann, Aunt Viola Helen, Uncle Patty, Uncle Charlie, Uncle Mike, Diane, Diana, Elyssa , Jen, Jessica , Donna and Anthony, Brian and Holly, Rob

I wanted to make you all a very special surprise this Christmas. I can't tell you sometimes in words how much I love you all. My heart can't contain all the love I have for you. Time, distance, and years have only made me realize how blessed I am to have you all in my life. The memories I share with all of you wrap around my heart like a warm blanket. I wanted to express in a very special way, how much your support has meant to me these last couple of years with me going thru all these health issues. Just as the earth goes through seasons, so does a family in the course of time endure seasons. Marriage, falling in love, and the birth of a children are times of renewal like spring. Long pleasant periods of calm that some families are blessed to have are like the feeling of an endless summer. As we and our children grow older, our leaves start to change. We start to experience autumn. This may seem like dying but it is really only signs of a new phase of life. The times of crises and hardship are times for the family to stay close together, help each other out and endure what are sometimes the frigid winds of change. This period is akin to winter. Life is full of seasons and changes which are best experienced with the support of friends and family. Friendship is a priceless gift .That can't be bought or sold, But its value is far greater, than a mountain made of gold. For gold is cold and lifeless, it cannot see nor hear, and in your times of trouble, it is powerless to cheer. It has no ears to listen, No heart to understand. It cannot bring you comfort, or reach out a helping hand. So when you ask God for a gift, be thankful that he sends, Not diamonds, pearls, or riches, But the love of a real, true friend. I wanted to send you a gift from the heart. A gift to make you smile forever. So as you flip through the pages of this book , no matter how far apart we are know I carry you in my heart, Now, Always and Forever more...

Love and God's Blessings,

Patti oxoxoxxox

My best friend Donna and I.... this was in 2008

Oh, this was also in 2008, I just came off my book signing tour in M.A, C.T and N.Y we came over your house to surprise you. You are showing the angels we got you.

Walking down the aisle at Brian and Holly's wedding. 2002

Me, Brian and our friends Anthony, Rob and Dawn. This was at Brian's birthday party.

Oh this was in Maine just a day before Sandy hit. This is when we were looking for houses up there.

Getting my party on in 2011 New Year's Eve...
APPLEBEES...

This was taken in Manorville on the night on Anthony's 45th birthday.

This was at a book signing in M.A.

Donna and I in 2009... We stopped at 711 for coffee. It was a freezing cold day in May. We had come up to N.Y. for a visit and we were not prepared for the cold. I had to buy a coat. Lol...

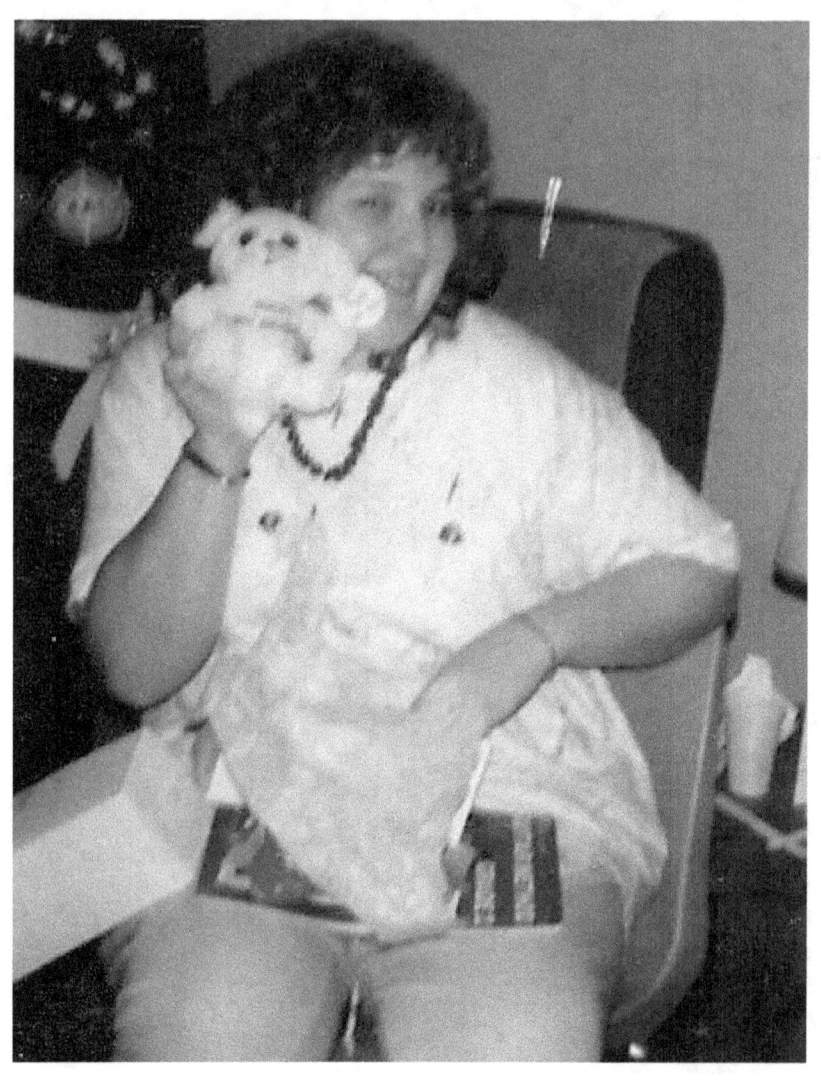

This was on my sweet 16...

Brian, Grandma and I on Grandma's birthday back in 1991.

Dad and I in Hoyt Farm 1976

The two drummers in 2008

03/10/2012

Mom and Anthony in 2012 we were at The Olive Garden for mom's birthday.

Road trip...

Book signing in 2008 in M.A.

Dinner with friends in 2008

Rob do you remember this? This was the night of the Def lap concert back in 92. I got food poisoning remember?

L.O.L. This is when we were driving to Long Island after Sandy we ran out of gas. We were on line for 3 days to get gas.

The boys working on the car.

Mom, Brian and Uncle Mike at Mom's 70th birthday party.

Grandma, Grandpa and Mom at the Sizzler 86... This was on Grandpa's birthday.

This was in N.J. On the boardwalk. This was a fun days. Oh how I wish we could go back to those days, when the family was all together. I miss you dad.

Anthony and I in 2007.

Dad and Brian. Brian always know dad is watching over you , even in Heaven. He loves us. He will always protect us. This was when we went to the Sizzler for Dad's birthday and yours.

Dad and Uncle Joe, the last time they were ever together. Sept 17, 2006. Weird that just days after this, dad was gone.

My 41st birthday in Manorville.

05/04/2008 06:31 PM

Mom, Aunt Mary and I in 2008. Aunt Mary and Mom you look so pretty in this picture.

Me at the Family Brick in the Lady of the
Shrine.

Anthony and I at Mom and Dad's house in Covington G.A. IN 2007. I think this was Christmas.

Awe. Anthony and our dog Lighting.(now gone) This picture was taken after Mom and Dad built on to Commack house for us. This was our 1st Christmas there. Lightning was such a good dog. He died of cancer.

My friends Anthony , dawn and I in 92.

This is a sweet picture from Anthony and I engagement party. Feb 14, 99

Grandma and Aunt Helen back in 1939...

Mom and I at a company Christmas Party.

Grandma fixing a bench.

Family visit in 2010☺

This was on my honey moon. This was the room at
the Sheraton.

Family Picnic late 1950s???

Dad and Grandma....

This is a bit hard to see but in this picture is, Me, Brian, Holly,) Holly's brother Erik, My best friend and Sister Donna and my good friend Rob. This was taken in 93 at a Christmas Party in Selden.

Ha, ha I surprised Holly when taking this picture.

Anthony and our dear friend Diana... in 2004
Diana we love and miss you. I know you are in
Heaven dancing with angels...

Grandma, Grandpa and Aunt Mary Christmas of 71....

Aunt Mary and I ... Love you Aunt Mary so much!
You are one of my heroes.

Could this be Aunt Maryann or Aunt Viola Helen? I found this picture in Grandma's papers.

This is a stunning shot. Taken at my 1st engagement party before I met Anthony.

10/20/2012

Anthony and I on our 13th Anniversary. This was taken at our church in G.A.

This is Grandma at work at the old lane's Dept.
Store in New Hyde Park. 1952...

AWE this was at Mom's 70th birthday in Manorville...

This was taken at a 50's style diner in F.L. Near Disney.

Mom and Anthony at the docks in Kings Park.

Anthony and I in N.J. In 2008

Mom and I in G.A. IN 2005

This is a bitter sweet picture. This was taken at the very last party we ever had in Commack in 2004.

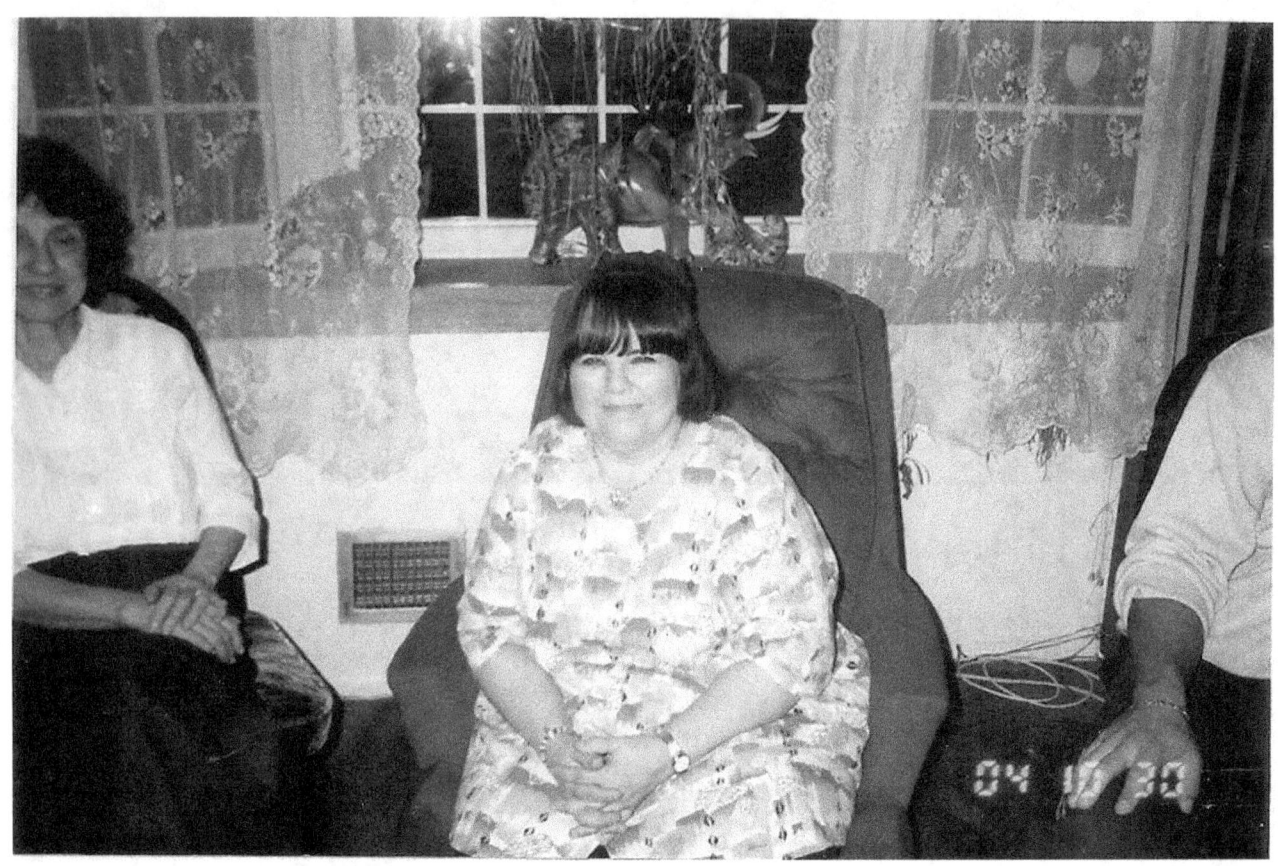

This was that same party...

Oh How I miss this house. How many great parties did we have there?

DAD AND I DON'T KNOW THE DOGGIES NAME..
55

Grandma and Mom and our doggie Thunder. This was on Thanksgiving 96

Again our last party in Commack....

AWE THIS IS A SWEET ONE... this was from the day Mom and Dad, Anthony and I all renewed our vows.

This was again in Commack. I tell you if I ever win the lotto I am buying my grandparents' house back!!!!!!!!

This is a funny shot, Brian and our friends Rob and Anthony comparing muscles!

I'm all ready for winter now!

Brian, Anthony and I in 2008 at Friendly's

Anthony surrounded by beautiful woman!

My H.S. Graduation day. June 1990

Brian and I on Mom and Dad's 25th wedding day...

Brian and Holly's wedding day

Were to sexy for this picture... L.O.L.

Brian and Holly way back in 84....

"To love another person is to touch the face of God"

Sweet Memories, Huh?

Love this one...

Aunt Helen and Grandma

Again at our going away party....

Brian with his friends Anthony and Dawn.. Back in 91 look how young they all look.

Don't mess with the law...

L.O.L. this was on the way up to N.Y. we stopped to do wash, I was bored so I snapped a picture....

Mom and I in 2008 On a trip to N.Y.

Another shot with friends...

"Friends are friends forever if the Lord is the Lord of them. A friend will not say never because the welcome never ends...."

GRANDPA SHOWING OFF HIS NEW CAR...

My graduation day...

Pretty in pink...

Does anyone know who these people are?
Found this in Grandma's photo book.

ANTHONY SO ROMANTIC.... F.L. 2009

Four handsome guys....

Dad, Grandma and Grandpa, Uncle Joe at Aunt
Viola's house....

Mom opening a Christmas gift....

This is on my 10ᵗʰ ann when Anthony and I renewed our vows...

The night before Brian and Holly's wedding....

This was taken at 1st engagement party before I knew Anthony...

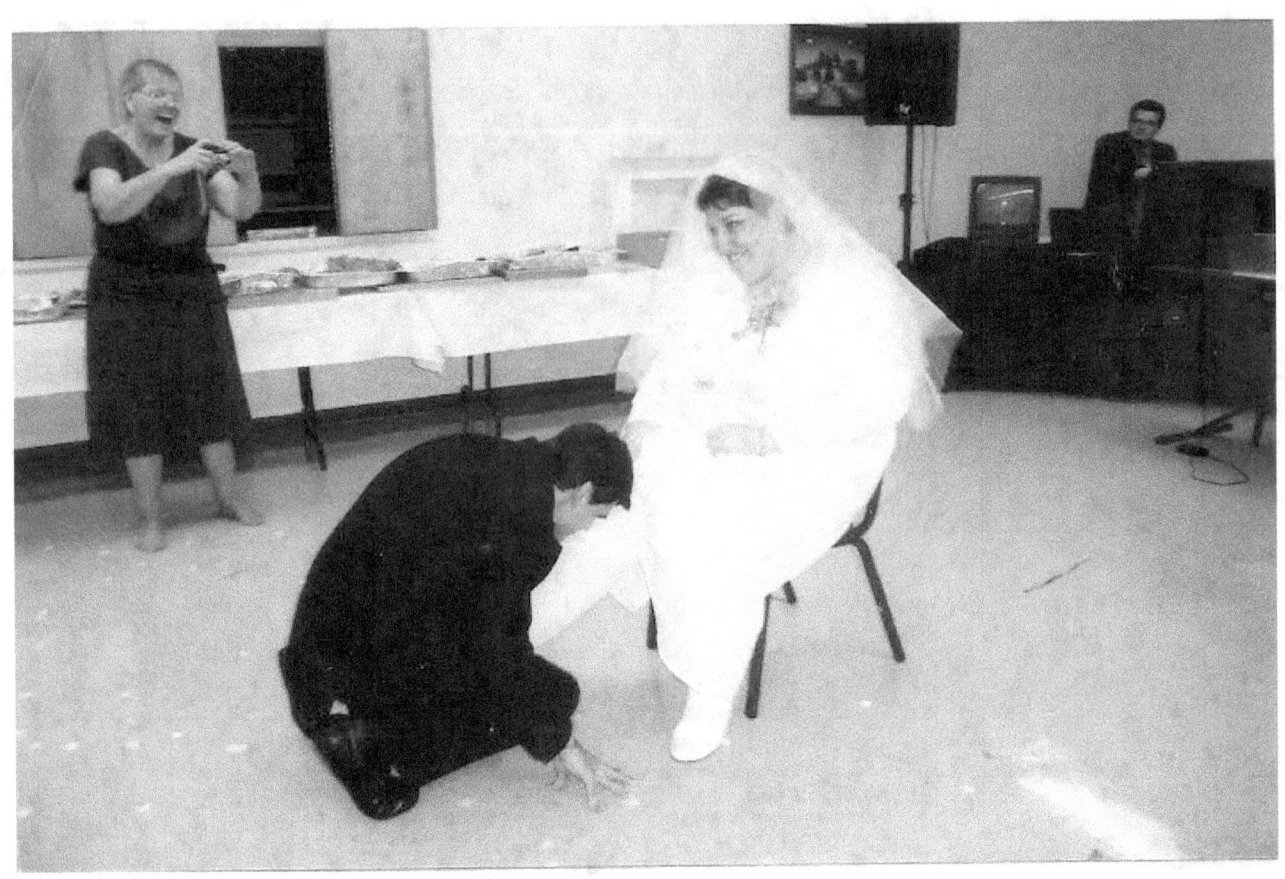

Our 10th WEDDING DAY....

Brian's prom day

Commack............

At my birthday

ANTHONY AND I AT Mom and Dad's house in
G.A. 2006

Grandma, Aunt Mary and I on my wedding day....

This was when we surprised you when I came to long Island for my book signing.. You said Uncle Pat got you the "Great Pumpkin" I love this picture of you....

Mama don't let your babies grow up to be cowboys.. G.A. 1ST THANKSGIVING THERE....

Halloween hay ride with friends 90

Easter... Mom, Dad and I

Dad's 1st Birthday in G.A.

Grandma and Grandpa at Cooky's in Smithtown 83

Another one I love from the wedding...

"Love one another as I have loved you."

AWE OUR DOGGIE Lighting.. 2009

Grandpa in his backyard...

These are the moments I cherish the most... To Love and be Loved is to feel the sun from both sides....

Fun in the sun...

Last party in Commack....

Grandma and Dad

Christmas 81

St Joe's in Kings park...

Our church in Leesburg.. Isn't it pretty....

From our Double renewal day...

Brian and I R.J.O. SCHOOL PARK, KINGS PARK...

O.k. this is an awesome picture. I had a book signing in C.T. that my publisher booked. My friend Anthony who I had not seen in 22 years surprised me. He came to the book signing cause he lived in that town but I didn't know he lived there or was coming... I met his girlfriend Dawn that day also they took Mom and I to dinner...

This is our doggie Smokey who jumps fences all the time. He's a sweetie...

Grandma, Aunt Viola and Great Grandma.. lady of the Island Shrine 62....

Is this Aunt Josephine? I'm sorry but I don't
know who this is....

My friend Rob and I at the prom...

My dancing days...

Mom and I in F.L. IN 2009 This was at a Botanical garden were they display over a million lights.

Wedding day fun...

When we bought our car.....

Grandma, Chris and John at the engagement party to my 1st fiancé....

On Grandma and Grandpa's 50th Ann....

Grandma, Aunt Viola and Great Grandma at the
Lady of the Island...

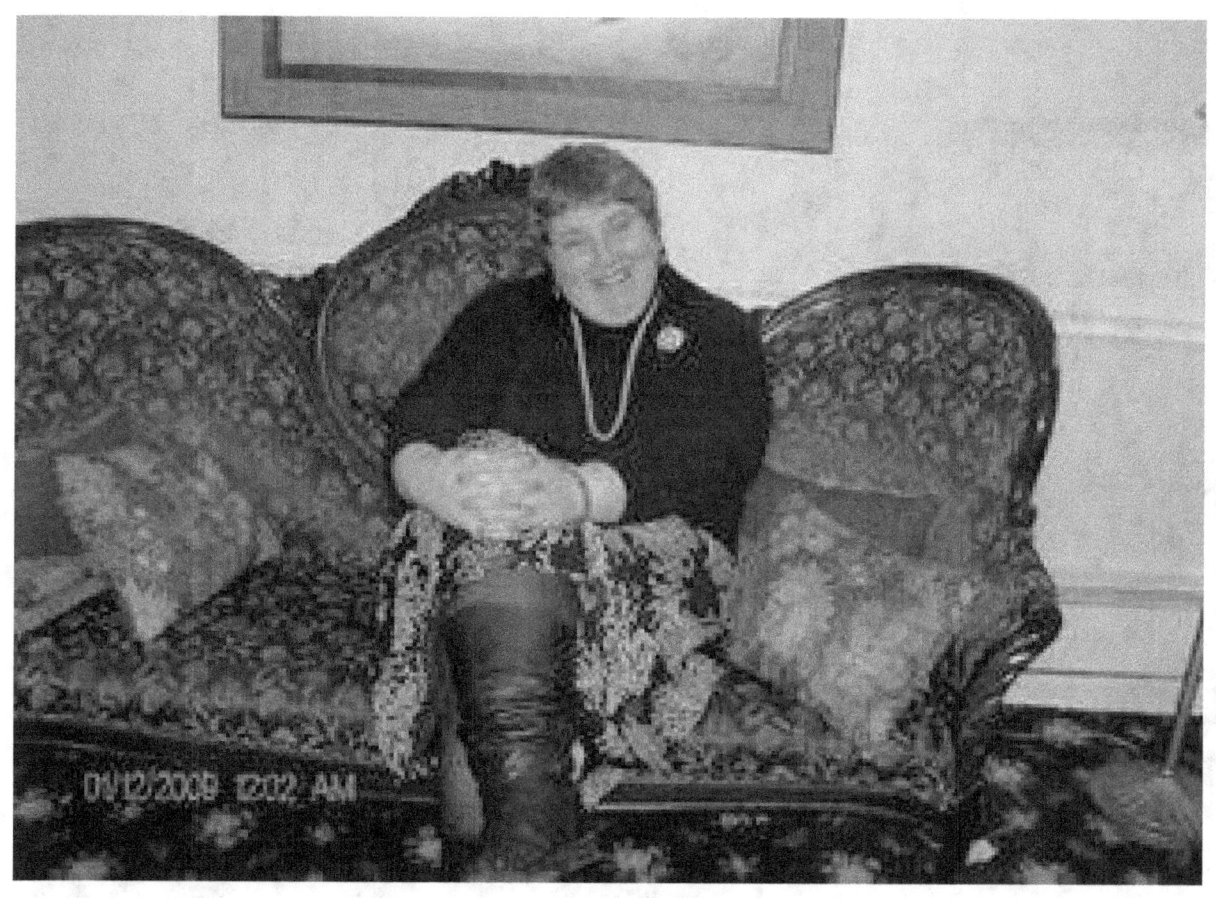

At a friend's shower... in 2009

Dad and Uncle Joe July 2004 In G.A.

Dad age 2 what a cutie..

Family fun in 78/79 New Years Eve

Billy from the band Firehouse and I...

Same day...

Rob, remember this day???

Mom, Dad, grandma and Grandpa in Selden...

Aunt Mary and Grandma and Baby Uncle Charlie??????

This was in New Orleans in 2012 my dear friend just gave me a make-over so I was showing off my new hair...

Party Time in Selden...

Grandma and Grandpa fooling around....

Dancing days....

Aunt Maryann???

Family visit... 2008

Grandma and dad I think....

New Years Eve in G.A.

Grandma

Dancing QUEEN...

Forever Family...

My modeling days....

Rock N Roll... My 18th Birthday.....

Brian and Anthony on way to City...

FAMILY DINNER AT Cooky's the day Brian and I made our Confirmation....

Being Silly....

Brian and his then friends ANTHONY...

Brian and I in 84...

Brain, Holly, Anthony and I IN 2012... I will love you forever, and take a bullet for anyone of you... Just know that....

Dad and Aunt Mary……. Such a sweet picture…

There are no words... to say how much I miss you dad, and Grandma...

05/04/2008 06:31 PM

Family fun 2008

Brian's prom... I will remember this day even when I forget my own name...

Ah, my 18ᵗʰ birthday…. Holly , my friend Dionne and I

DAD

Christmas time 90

My friend Rob...

Grandma and Dad

The Boys....

Family dinner

My 18th birthday

Mom and Snoopy in a park in F.l.

Grandma, Brian and I

Uncle Pat and I dancing to "In the Mood."

Mom in N.J....

Grandma and Grandpa on Thanksgiving...

Mom, Dad, Thunder and I......

My friend Anthony and I in the park... we were re-living our childhood.

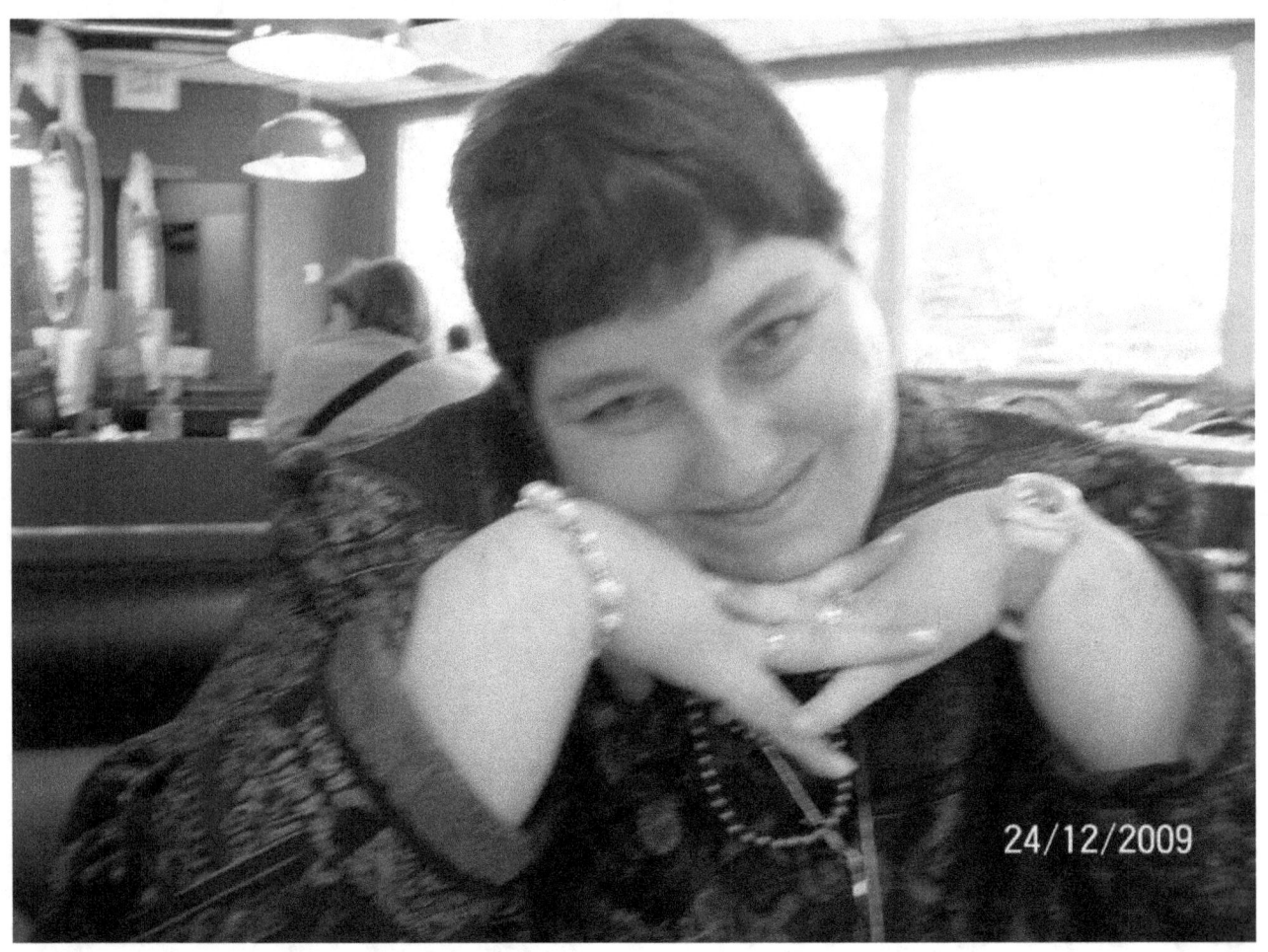

24/12/2009

Being silly in 2009........

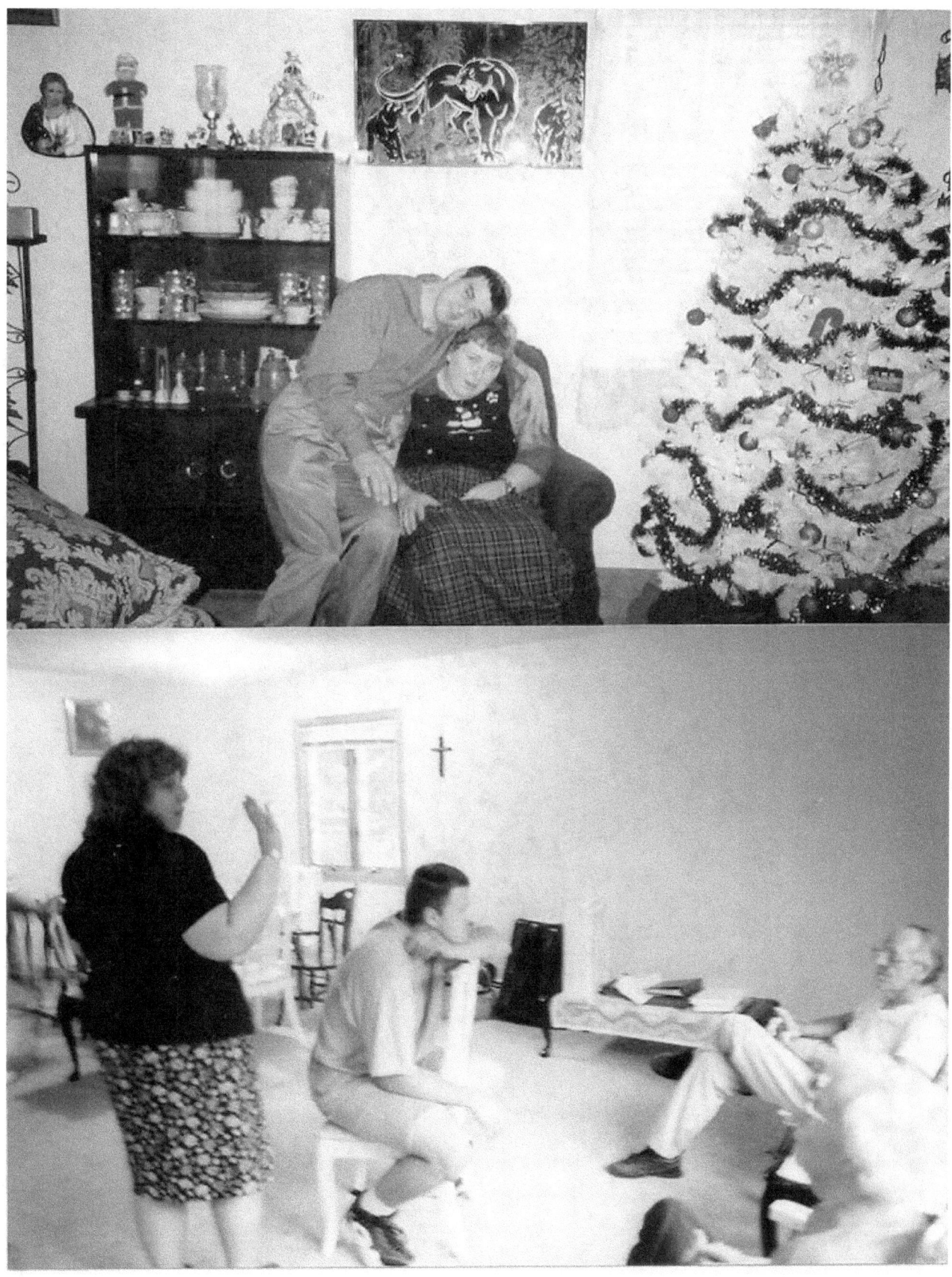

Christmas memories....

Christmas Party in Commack....

2003....

Holly's wedding day...

Mom and I the day we went to see Phantom Of the Opera…. I love the book, play and Gerry☺

Dad just a few weeks before he passed.. at my house in G.A.

Our pretty girl snoopy she is now 15 years
old... isn't she pretty???

Lady of the Island.. dad, Great Grandma(grandpa's mom) grandpa...

My Wedding Shower...

Anthony and I date night 2010

Our family brick at the Lady of the Island shrine...

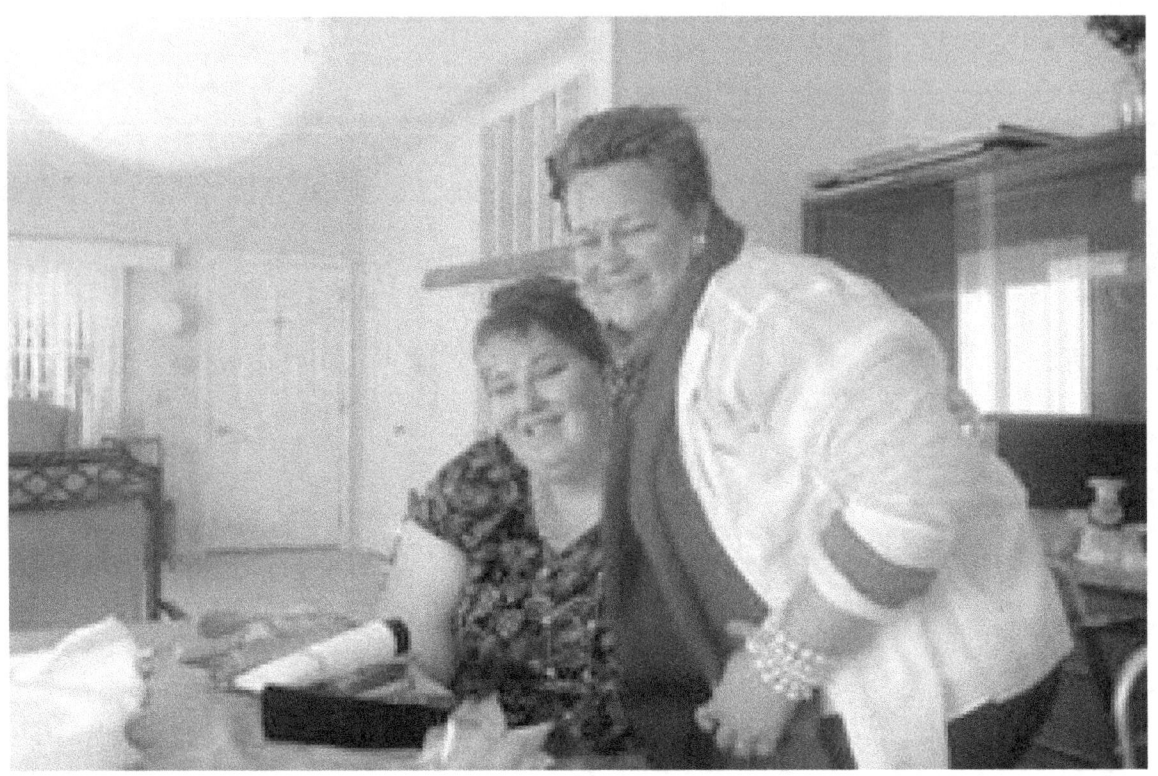

My best friend Donna and I

Hard to see but My hair was pink in this pic.. I dyed it for Breast Cancer awareness....

Dinner with friends at the Candlelight...

Disney with the girls

Halloween.. Anthony and I dressed as Crazy escaped Mental people from K.P.......

Me, Mom and My other best friend Stevi from New Orleans....

My best friend Stevi and I

K.F.C. DAY...

He's in the Army now... Grandpa you make us so proud... Thank you for fighting for our Freedom....

AGAIN MY FRIEND Stevi and I in New Orleans(where she lives)

This was right before our double renewal picking up the cake...

Having fun on our 1st trip to F.L.

Left to right... Aunt Barbara, Mom, uncle Joe, my sister in law Christen, Jocelyn(my niece) Dad, Brian , me, my niece Kassidy, Anthony's mom, Than, Margaret, and their kids.... On my front lawn in G.A. Taken just weeks before dad passed. Brian surprised us by coming down and Anthony's family were down on a planned trip... I think God planned it for us all to be together...

God 1st praying before we eat...

Hard at work on another novel....

My birthday in Manorville

AGAIN IN New Orleans

At our Engagement Party...

Smokey has a bone..

Road trip lunch stop ...

Anthony's 40th birthday

The day we met Scrooge...

07/05/2010

Donna and I

Wedding

Anthony, Donna and I

This is our living room in leesburg....

Brian got a new racetrack....

Mom and Dad at a friend's wedding...

Aw very handsome Uncle Willie....

I hope you all enjoyed this walk down memory lane. I love you all. Let us take a moment to reflect and pray for those who are no longer with us...Our Father,

We acknowledge you as the creator of family. Thank you for our mother, father, brothers, sisters, aunts, uncles, cousins, and grandparents.

We believe in your promises and desire to apply your truth. Thank you for being faithful even when we are not.

We trust you will provide us with a well deep enough to love each other without end. Thank you that you loved us first.

We confess that we have not always treated our family with kindness. Thank you for showing us the path to forgiveness.

Protect our marriage from those who wish to destroy. Guard our children from those who wish to harm. Deliver us from hands that meddle and mouths that gossip.

If we desire children but have none, give us patience and hope. If we are without a spouse, give us strength and companionship. If we have lost too soon, give us peace and comfort.

Let our words be used to build up and encourage one another. Let our actions glorify and exalt you.

Grant us wisdom to recognize your voice and the courage to answer it.

We pledge our family to love. We pledge our family to truth. We pledge our family to you, Lord.

For those in our family who do not know you, we pray for their salvation. For those in our family who have gone astray, we pray for their return.

You have put us together for a purpose. We desire for that purpose to be known so that our feet may be put into action.

Allow our family to be a beacon of light that shines brightly in this dark world. Allow our family the opportunity to pursue others as you pursued us.

Thank you for your love. Thank you for giving us one another. Thank you for the family.

Love always,

Patti

www.ingramcontent.com/pod-product-compliance
Lightning Source LLC
Chambersburg PA
CBHW081059290526
45795CB00006B/1926